Festivals with children

Brigitte Barz

Festivals with children

Floris Books

Translated by James and Cynthia Hindes

First published in German under the title
Feiern der Jahresfeste mit Kindern
by Verlag Urachhaus, Stuttgart, 1984.
First published in English in 1987 by Floris Books.

British Library CIP Data

Barz, Brigette
Festivals with children.
1. Fast and feasts
I. Title   II. Feiern der Jahresfeste mit Kindern. *English*
263'.9   BV30

ISBN 0-86315-055-1

Printed in Great Britain
by Billing & Sons Ltd, Worcester

Contents

Introduction

The festivals are nodal points of the year which unite us with the Spirit of the Universe.
                                    Rudolf Steiner

The Christian festivals are an indispensable part of the religious education of the child. When properly celebrated they provide indispensable nourishment for the soul. However, much of the content of the Christian festivals, cannot and should not be brought directly to the child. Abstract intellectual explanations must be avoided if the pictures and symbols in festival celebrations are to acquire importance as living experiences for the children. Every custom and symbol must be as genuine as possible, must be able to honestly express something of the essence of that particular festival. Through the centuries a wealth of customs of varying quality have been developed and passed on. Many of them are described in this book and some new ones have been added. Yet, the reader should not merely accept these descriptions as simple prescriptions. An idea or experience conveyed by symbols, actions or customs must be understood by the adults involved before it can become a living experience for the children. The question concerning its 'golden background', the reasons for its existence must be asked. This book is especially concerned with such 'reasons'.

The success of a festival depends, not so much on the wealth of possibilities for shaping it, but rather on how the parents participate. Everything which they themselves do or which they have the children do must be accompanied by genuine feeling. We must strive to immerse ourselves anew in the meaning of the festival to bring it to life within. Then we are creating and building on a golden foundation of truthfulness, the only basis upon which we should ever do such anything for children.

If we are successful in elevating and warming the hearts of the children at the nodal points of the year, at the Christian festivals, they will be blessed with the touch of him whose working into the present we celebrate in these festivals.

I would like to express my gratitude to the teachers and parents whose work I am allowed to share, who for years tested these ideas in everyday practice. They have been a great help to me.

1 Basics elements of festivals

There are several elements which have a necessary place at every festival. Only the 'dress' in which they appear will change according to the nature of the festival. These fundamental elements include:

The table

A small table, chest of drawers, trunk or even a box with a special broad board upon it are all suitable for a festival or season's table.*

It is best if it has its own special place in the home, not to be used by the children for their everyday play. During the times not dedicated to any particular festival, it can serve as a place for bringing nature into the house. Flowers and other things found or crafted by the children have their place of honor here.

The cloth

The table can be covered with a cloth the color of which should change with the time of year. Green is a good color for much of the year.

---

* This idea was originally suggested by Friedel Lenz in *Celebrating Festivals with Children*.

The picture

Every festival has its own special picture. The content of this picture should have a direct bearing on the current festival. Finding a suitable picture from the wealth of ancient or recent works of art can be an enjoyable task. Art calendars are often particularly useful in the search for just the 'right' picture. Otherwise art postcards can be glued to a piece of colored cardboard or attached to a cloth. Specific suggestions as to color will be given in the later chapters. If the festival table stands next to a wall, the picture can hang above it.

Nature

Every festival time has its own special place in the course of the year. Therefore, nature should always be included with an appropriate bouquet. In some seasons, for example, at St John's Tide, flowers play a central role in the symbolism of the festival. A few beautifully arranged flowers or branches are often more meaningful than an overwhelming abundance.

The candle

A candle should be lighted for every celebration in the home no matter how small. A burning candle is an external sign for the inner experience of light and warmth which we want to awaken in this festive moment; therefore the candle has a definite place on the festival table. The experience of light stands in the foreground of many festivals, for example at Advent, Christmas, Epiphany, and Whitsun, which will be described in detail later.

Poems and songs

There are appropriate songs and verses for every festival season. Here also, guided by our feelings and insights we need to make choices. Small children listen as something is read to them or spoken for them by older siblings or grown-ups. Gradually, the child will find joy in speaking or singing along. Very likely children in school will have learned some songs and verses and be able to contribute to the celebration. Here, again it is not the quantity which is important. Less can be more! Music, in a house where it is cultivated, provides a natural means of enriching the festival. And an upcoming festival can become an incentive to practice!

The festival story

Almost all the festivals discussed here have an appropriate story from the Gospels. Pre-schoolers can listen when parents read aloud to the older siblings. If a reading from the Gospel is chosen, then it must be well prepared.

One will also find many suitable stories in fairy tales, especially those of the Brothers Grimm. Most are not obviously attributable to any one particular season; however with an increasing understanding of the meaning of the festival and the fairy tales themselves, we can gradually acquire confidence in choosing which story to read. As always, it is important for the storyteller to maintain in his heart the impulse which leads to the choice. Many suggestions for choices will be given in later chapters.

Generally speaking, legends are only suitable for children from the second school year on. Whether one reads the stories in the morning or evening will depend upon the festival itself and upon the family situation.

2 Advent

The word Advent comes from the Latin word *advenir* which means 'to arrive'. Advent is a time of preparation; for children in particular it is the time of joyful anticipation which seeks and finds its fulfillment at Christmas.

During Advent our thoughts and feelings of thankfulness go in two directions. Looking back to the past we are reminded of the world Advent, of the great hopes of the world for the arrival of a savior. All the great pre-Christian religions awaited a redeemer. The records which have been passed down from various cultures constitute a wonderful picture, a prophetic preview of the working of Christ. Of course, the expectation of a savior lived most clearly in the Israelites and is expressed in the Old Testament. We all have good reason to remember with deep gratitude the historical Advent and fits fulfillment, but our glance should also go in the other direction. Advent is also a festival of the present and of the future. Before Christ's life on earth ended on Golgotha, he gave his disciples the promise of his return, as stated in the Gospels in Matthew 24, Mark 13, Luke 21, and in various letters in the

New Testament. Christ's return to mankind will not occur again in an earthly body. Emil Bock once formulated this as follows, 'Once he came in being; that was the Christmas experience two thousand years ago. Now, however, he will come in consciousness. That is the Christmas experience which is intended for our age.'

Every year the Advent season, which in earlier ages was a serious time of fasting, can be a stimulation to discipline and exercise ourselves inwardly in order to grow toward the second Coming. The Greek word *parusia*, which is usually translated with the words, 'second coming', also means 'presence', 'being with', 'present'. Christ is always here! The last sentence in Matthew's Gospel reads, 'I am with you always, to the close of the age.' Understood in this way, the Second Coming shows us there are many stages of experience and degrees of perception of this closeness.

In the season of Advent one word wants to be heard in every human soul: the word 'become'. And there is an image which corresponds to this word: Mary on the path toward the birth at Christmas: 'Behold — the handmaid of the Lord; let it be to me according to your word' (Luke 1:38). Mary is not only a historical person. She is also an archetype of the human soul's willingness 'to become', to grow and prepare for the birth of that which wants to come. This is visible even in the clothing she wears: in the cloak of blue which surrounds and protects and in the warmth of the red shining forth from within.

> 'I must become like Mary, and bring forth
>   God in me
> If he should grant me blessedness for all
>   eternity.'
>
> Angelus Silesius

The calm and quiet which is a prerequisite for every 'inner becoming' is under attack everywhere today but especially during Advent. Today it can only be achieved through conscious effort.

There are so many customs and suggestions for the celebration of Advent that we must choose consciously to meet our particular situation. This period of time is in danger of losing its own characteristic mood. The atmosphere of preparation is often overwhelmed by the Christmas mood of fulfillment itself. Children have often already had enough by Christmas. Too often Christmas Eve is experienced as a hard-to-achieve climax followed by exhaustion making the celebration of the twelve days of Christmas very difficult.

Of the many suggestions for celebrating Advent we will suggest a few here, which, in their symbolism, contain something of the 'becoming'. This season needs a fullness which can slowly be intensified without achieving a complete state of fulfillment.

The festival table

The special color for Advent is blue, like Mary's cloak, and the color of dusk and dawn. Therefore blue material serves as a background for the table. The basic elements are a picture of the annunciation of the archangel Gabriel to Mary, and the Advent wreath.

The Advent wreath

Though wreath and circle are ancient symbols, the origin of the Advent wreath is much more recent. It is a custom from the end of the nineteenth century which spread quickly. Its origin most likely was in a house for the care and education of youth in the proximity of Hamburg. At that time it probably had twenty-four candles, one for each day of December. Today an Advent wreath has four candles. On each of the four Sundays of Advent one more candle is lit. While the external sunlight is diminishing the child can experience an increasing fullness of light with the approach of Christmas. On the Saturday before the first Advent Sunday a wonderful atmosphere can arise while the family makes one or more Advent wreaths. A child who can watch the binding of a wreath made from fresh branches, smell the air filled with evergreen fragrance and, with time, be allowed to help himself, is given an experience of childhood which will never be forgotten.

The celebration of Advent

Advent presents an opportunity to practice the celebration of Christian festivals at home. An atmosphere of joyful expectation is quickly awakened with the lighting of a candle when the quiet and darkness have been experienced by the children for a few moments. This experience can be deepened by the delicate tones of a kantele, lyre or other instrument or the humming of an Advent song which gradually fills the room. For children who are old enough we can read the Advent Gospel from Luke (1:26–38). Singing, speaking a poem and making music together can provide both a conclusion for the little festival and a transition to a contemplative hour. In such hours the older children are especially open for heart to heart conversations. A bowl with fruit and nuts will be very welcome. The results of Christmas baking should be saved for the twelve days of Christmas for the reasons already indicated. Self-restraint is an important achievement during Advent.

Small children have an astonishing ability to enter quickly and entirely into the mood of Advent and Christmas. Many parents immerse themselves in the mood of their children and allow themselves to be carried by it. Hence, the sad and regrettable comment of many present-day adults: 'I can only celebrate Advent and Christmas with small children.' We should not allow this to happen. We must bring our own inner activity to prepare the Advent and Christmas festivals in order to celebrate them anew each year.

As the children become older it is no longer so easy to find the childlike joy of the Advent mood. It is then good to relate the celebration more to the present-day Advent. The three parables found in Chapter 25 of Matthew's Gospel (the ten virgins, the ten talents, and the last judgment) are also Advent Gospels. They come from Christ and are intended to prepare us for his second coming. The beautiful story by Tolstoy, 'Where Love Is, There Is God', also takes up the themes of this chapter. Another good activity for parents and older children is studying together paintings of Advent themes. This often awakens a warm regard for the paintings. The joyful discovery of individual visual and symbolic motifs easily leads to a conversation. From the wealth of literature for Advent there are stories which, when broken up into smaller parts, are well suited to enriching the Sundays of Advent. Every family will eventually find their 'own' story.

The time before Christmas is interwoven with mysteries. Beautiful memories are created in the hours we spend within the family circle creating together, whether ornaments for Advent and Christmas or little gifts for others. Practical helps for this are found in the very valuable book, *Advent for Children* by Freya Jaffke.

The Advent calendar

Small children hardly have any sense of time or duration. The many types of Advent calendars described in Jaffke's book enable us to increase their sense of time by making its passage visible. Day by day fulfillment draws closer, and it gradually becomes Christmas. For small children the simplest and most appropriate Advent calendar is the Carpet of Stars. Every morning one star more appears on the blue cloth over the festival table. Straw or gold stars are particularly well suited. At Christmas this carpet of stars can provide the background for the manger.

If we have the Mary figure walk gradually toward the manger through the days of Advent, each daily step can be represented with a little star. Her path then appears as a starry trail behind her. Great care must be exercised with Advent calendars 'filled' with little daily surprises that they do not become the fulfillment themselves. Without intending to, we often awaken a child's greed through such calendars. It makes more sense to make a filled calendar for the twelve days of Christmas.

The manger scene

'For the creation waits with eager longing for the revealing of the Sons of God.' (Rom.8:19)

The kingdoms of nature — stone, plant and animal — which, through man 's fall into sin, have themselves fallen from the paradisal existence are waiting for the becoming of man, of the sons of God, in order to find their own salvation through that of man. We have reason to be deeply thankful for the sacrifice which these kingdoms have brought and continue to bring to us. The poem by Christian Morgenstern, 'The Washing of the Feet' expresses this gratitude.

The Washing of the Feet

I thank you, silent stone on earth,
and gently lean to you below.
My life as plant I owe to you.

I thank you, grounds and meadows green
and bend down close to you below.
My life as animal depends on you.

I thank you animal, and plant, and stone,
And bow down thankfully to you below.
You helped me to become, all three.

And we thank you, you child of man,
And kneel in reverence before you:
Only because you are, are we.

From all of God 's creation, simple
or so manifold, rise thanks.
In thankfulness all being intertwines.

Rudolf Frieling associates the four kingdoms of nature with the four Sundays of Advent.* 'To begin with there is the fourfoldness of the Sundays of Advent. Four is the number of the world in which we usually stand, the world as it has become today. Beneath all is the kingdom of the inert stones, of the dead inorganic matter. There upon is built the kingdom of the living plants. Above that stands the kingdom of the animals. And finally, all is crowned by the kingdom of man to the extent that he has appeared in the course of world evolution. That is "our" world.'

We can reflect these thoughts in shaping the manger scene; we expand the scene by one

* *Das heilige Spiel.*

kingdom on each of the four Sundays. A green table provides the background. On the first Sunday stones and crystals of varying size are placed upon it. The children can bring the most precious 'treasures' they have for the manger. On the second Sunday we add what the plant kingdom has to offer: moss, pine cones, dried flowers from St John's Tide, even small roses are all welcome. Together with the stones they create a landscape. In this landscape the animal finds its place on the third Sunday, from snail and sea shells, perhaps even a piece of honeycomb, to animals handcrafted out of beeswax. The shepherd's sheep can also graze here. On the fourth Sunday the shepherds appear and build the stall as a cave or house. The entire manger scene may not all fit on the festival table. In any case it should be placed where the children can always see it.

Another possibility for the shaping of the manger scene is to place the four kingdoms of nature in sequence on steps. Each step receives its own kingdom. The landscape is best for small children, the steps for older children. Even adults for their own celebration might like to arrange the four kingdoms of nature, without a manger scene.

St Barbara's branches

The fourth of December is St Barbara's Day. It is the anniversary of the death of the early Christian martyr (AD 306) who, because of her faith, was locked by her father in a tower which has become her symbol. She was later beheaded. The custom of cutting 'Barbara' branches on this day has gradually arisen over the centuries. Strangely enough there is no legend upon which this custom is based. We must seek its source elsewhere.

Age old wisdom sets the beginning of winter on November 23. Twelve days later on December 4 a turning point has arrived for the invisible life processes of the earth and plants. In earlier times one knew about the forces present on this day and made use of them in order to have fresh green branches twenty–one days later at Christmas. This process in the forces of life combined with the memorial day for the martyr have led to the custom of 'Barbara branches'.

Rudolf Steiner said: '. . . and in many souls there arose something of a feeling for the life that can never be conquered, the life which will be the victor over all death when the carefully gathered shoots or branches of trees stand in a festive way in the room during the Christmas night and are unnaturally brought to blossom in the night when the sun is at its lowest

point.'* Particularly suitable for Barbara branches are cherry, apple, plum, almond, for-
sythias, jasmine and horse chestnut. They
should be placed in lukewarm water overnight
and then in a vase with water in a warm room.
The water should be changed every three days.
Occasional misting is recommended. When the
branches later stand near the manger, the children will be able to watch how they open — a
wonderful 'Christmas sermon'.

Preparation of gifts

The background for the custom of making
gifts at Christmas is this: the love which should
accompany every present is a reflection of the
love which flows from the divine and is also an
expression of our connection to God.

A gift becomes a genuine Christmas present
when it calls forth joy, warmth and love in the
recipient, helping to bring him into the proper
mood of Christmas. This is most readily
achieved through carefully and lovingly chosen
personal 'signs' — even of a purely ideal sort —
rather than through expensive objects. Advent
offers a wonderful opportunity to introduce
children to the careful and loving preparation
(even the wrappings) of presents. If the child's
own preparation of little presents is filled with

* *Festivals of the Seasons*, p.36 (1909 Dec 21), (retranslated here).

joy, warmth and love for the recipient, then the child feels enriched himself. That is a genuine preparation for Christmas. For every Christmas present should maintain its connection with the great Christmas gift that has come to us all and is renewed every Christmas. 'In this the love of God was made manifest among us, that God sent his only son into the world so that we might live through him' (1John 4:9).

3 Christmas

'For to you is born today . . . a Saviour' (Luke 2:11). So reads the first joyful Christmas message of the world from the angel of the Lord to the shepherds in the fields.

This 'today' bears within it, as do so many other 'todays' in the Gospel, the character of something which is eternally applicable. We can renew the impulse to celebrate Christmas by contemplating the eternal fact which, at every Christmas time, wants to become a new event for mankind.

In the pre-Christian societies of northern Europe which were guided by mystery centers the birth of all children was carefully arranged to take place during the days which are now known as the twelve days of Christmas. Through carefully protected institutions the purity of conception was guarded. The first-born son, that is, the first son born during these days was later entrusted with great tasks. Today we should bear in mind the fact that during these days a spiritual birth takes place in the soul of man.

'If Christ is born a thousand times in
    Bethlehem
and not in you, you remain eternally lost.'
                                    Angelus Silesius

The days around the winter solstice which have
become the time to celebrate Christmas had an
important significance in many pre-Christian
religions. During this time the victory of light
over darkness was celebrated, for example, in
the Egyptian, Teutonic, Jewish, Celtic,
Roman, and the Mithras religions.

It was only in the fourth century that Christmas began to be celebrated on December 25.
Until then the most important day of celebration was January 6, the day of the Baptism of
Jesus in the Jordan, the day of Christ's actual
incarnation upon earth in Jesus. There may
have been external reasons for this shift of day,
but the essential reason was the early
Christian's feeling that every year anew during
the days between December 24 and January 6 a
special stream of blessing flowed into earth
existence.

In addition to looking backwards at the
events of Christmas 'then', at the birth of the
Jesus child in the stall in Bethlehem, parents
should also acquire an inner relationship to
Christmas 'today'. Our celebration of this festival with the children should always take into
account this double aspect. It is clear from the

Christmas story (Luke 2:1–20), even down to the formulations of the words, that the Christmas happening is an event in space and time ('In those days . . . the time came for her to be delivered . . . there was no place for them in the inn'). Preparing the house for Christmas should be a sign that we are prepared to give a space in us for Christmas. The fulfillment of this time is prepared through the celebration of Advent.

The manger scene

There was a time when manger scenes were found only in churches. Today, however, the manger scene has an important place wherever Christmas is celebrated with children. Although historical events are represented through the figures, they also can become a picture for what happens at Christmas time today. We can experience something in the figures of the manger scene which corresponds to something in us.

Mary: An archetype for the human soul which is prepared to grow and become.
Joseph: Sometimes also called the protecting, caring 'foster father', Joseph can represent the bodily nature of man, that is, the earthly, physical foundation for existence on the earth.
The shepherds: They watch over those creatures needing protection which have been

entrusted to them. They are open to the words
of the angel, representatives of inner wakefulness, of openness for the divine, of the heart's
powers of devotion and reverence. Out of
genuine humility they can worship 'the child'.
The ox and the ass: Although the ox and the ass
do not appear in Luke's Christmas story, they
have had a place in the manger scene for a long
time. Here, we can think of the quote from the
prophet Isaiah (1:3), 'The ox knows its owner,
and the ass its master's crib; but Israel does not
know, my people does not understand.' The
ox and the ass can become an admonition for us
not to allow the events of Christmas to pass us
by without recognizing what is happening and
consciously seeking to understand these
events.
The Child: Born at the first Christmas, the child
must be born again within us, as Angelus
Silesius said. According to Rudolf Steiner, he is
the 'child of the spirit in the womb of the soul'.

The book *Advent for Children* by Freya Jaffke,
has many useful suggestions for beautiful man-
gers which are easy to make, even for inex-
perienced hands.
   Every child is capable of developing an
intimate affinity with the individual figures of
the manger scene. Able to identify with them
all, he would also be glad to act Mary, Joseph
or a shepherd in a play. Some families have

begun a tradition of acting out manger scenes with members of the family filling all the roles. This is done not for performance but for their own enjoyment using the simplest props and dividing the roles up differently each time. In smaller families one person must often take more than one role. The children then live with these pictures through the entire Christmas time.

The Christmas tree

December 24 is also Adam and Eve Day. In many places in earlier centuries 'paradise plays' were performed on this day. Plays in which the creation of man and the fall into sin were portrayed with powerful pictures deeply affected the souls of the onlookers. The beginning of mankind's suffering and the beginning of the salvation through the birth of Christ are brought together in a significant way by the association of Adam and Eve with the day preceding Christmas. In these plays a 'paradise' tree of pine or fir with apples was shown to the people as the forbidden Tree of Knowledge. Here we have the origin of the Christmas tree, first mentioned in a document from 1605. It is, however, certainly much older.*

---

* More on the history in *Der Weihnachtsbaum und seine Heimat, das Elsass*, by C. Schneider.

The paradise tree is the tree of the first Adam. Therefore, it is sometimes called Adam's tree. The apostle Paul describes Christ as the new Adam (Rom.5:12–21; 1Cor.15:21–49). The tree of the new Adam is the cross on Golgotha.

The Christmas tree stands between both. The path which leads the Son of God to the salvation of all mankind begins at Christmas and so we decorate the tree with the signs and symbols which represent this new beginning.

For a Christmas tree, a pine or fir tree is preferable. Of course, in some countries a different tree will have to be chosen. The green needles of a fir or pine tree in the depth of winter provide evidence of the life which always continues. The stern, clear form of the trunk, clearly accentuating the vertical and upright, and the horizontal spread of the branches already allow us to feel something of the cross.

The ornamentation of a Christmas tree should not be excessive, and it should help to express the symbolic essence of the tree. The earliest decorations consisted of apples, paper roses and baked goods. The apples remind us of the tree of paradise. The Latin word *malum* means at the same time 'apple' and 'evil'. Many locations also had the custom of hanging carved wooden figures of Adam, Eve and the snake on the tree.

'The roses that grow from the green are a symbol of the victory of the eternal over the temporal.'* Roses are easy to make out of tissue paper. A good number would be thirty-three which is thirty plus three. Jesus was baptized at age thirty. For three years after the Baptism in the Jordan, the Son of God lived in a human body on earth. So thirty-three red or thirty red and three white roses are a significant total. The roses should be placed as far out on the tips of the branches as possible.

Candles were added to the tree only later. Today we can no longer imagine the tree without lights. 'Light is love', Christian Morgenstern once said. The secret of light is contained in that sentence. Much can be thought and written about light, but it should be obvious that the lights on the Christmas tree are an expression of divine love, which

Who lights the candles? On Christmas Eve appeared in Christ on the earth and can stream to us anew particularly every Christmas time. the children are led to the tree which is already lit. In the ensuing days of Christmas it could be continued in this way. Perhaps, however, the children could also be allowed to experience the lighting of the candles. Then, the Christmas light is at the same time an answer;

* Rudolf Steiner, *Signs and Symbols of the Christmas Festival*, p.59 (1906 Dec 17), (Retranslated here.)

the answer of human love to the call of divine love.

Baked goods on the Christmas tree. The first Christmas trees bore small round breads. Just as the apples on the Christmas tree are a reminder of the Tree of Knowledge, so the bread is a reminder of the new life which the new Adam brings to man. We can adopt this old custom transforming it in a special way for the children. Something specially baked and not served elsewhere is hung upon the tree; at the conclusion of every evening around the tree, one can be taken down for each person and eaten. The next morning the 'sweet bread' mysteriously appears anew on the tree. In this way the Christmas tree stands before the children: blossoming, shining, bestowing.

Every family will decorate 'their' Christmas tree in their own way. One could certainly add many other things, for example, straw stars. But, always, the question should be asked: What is the meaning? What is the golden background of any particular custom? Not everything which can be hung is suitable as an ornament. Otherwise the beautiful symbol of the Christmas tree is transformed into a mere decoration for the living room.*

* If the symbols suggested by Rudolf Steiner for the tree are put up, it should not be done without a knowledge of the background. This can read, for instance, in *Signs and Symbols of the Christmas Festival*, (1906 Dec 17).

Father Christmas

In the English-speaking countries the tradition of Father Christmas is strong. He is not St Nicholas the bishop, who in America, following the Dutch name of Sinterklaas is called Santa Claus. In some American families he brings not only gifts to fill the stockings, but others as well. This kind old man with the long beard is age-old like the forces that lie at the basis of all that exists. He comes from the depths of time like the powers that carry the mountains and the wide seas. On Christmas night he brings gifts to the children, and leaves these in their stockings or shoes. Both are wrappings of our feet which, even today in our mobile age, still carry us on our path through life into our future destiny. Father Christmas brings gifts for the future 'on the way'. He puts weight into their stockings and so helps to strengthen the children's relationship with the earth.*

The twelve days of Christmas

Already in pre-Christian times it was felt that the days between December 25 and January 6 were permeated with a special quality. They

* Marta Heimeran described more of the background of Father Christmas in *The Christmas Community*, December 1934.

represent the difference between the year calculated according to the moon rhythm (354 days) and the sun year (365 days).

In his study of time and rhythms, Wilhelm Hoerner explains: 'The difference between the sun and the moon years consists of eleven, in leap years twelve, days. If January 6 is a new moon, then on December 25 a moon year with twelve full lunar cycles will have been completed. Then only the twelve days are lacking to the completion of a full sun year. Those days were added to December 25 by the northern peoples in order to bring the moon year into agreement with the sun year. On these days, which were dedicated to the gods, no heavy work was to be done. The human being was able to experience a conscious unity with higher worlds. Many practices, rules and regulations still give a faint echo of these "holy nights", of which the words "the twelve days of Christmas" are now only a remnant. On New Year's Eve the noise made at midnight reminds us of noise once made to drive out the demons. The twelve days were seen as prophetic for the twelve months of the coming year. Our New Year's Day falls in the middle of this time of "holy nights". For those wishing to live truly consciously these twelve days and thirteen (including Christmas Eve) nights can become a "time set apart", in which reflection and prayer have a special place, in a manner similar to the seven days of Holy Week.'

Those who were careful to celebrate Advent only as a time of preparation will find they can celebrate Christmas with the children as a time of fulfillment. The inwardness and warmth of these days are among the most precious childhood memories for innumerable people. On each of these twelve days time should be found for gathering around the Christmas tree and the manger, even if only for a short while. A Christmas story can be told, perhaps a different one each day if the children are older. The retelling of such stories from year to year is eagerly anticipated. Singing and playing musical instruments, the reciting of a poem or verse, can all contribute to the making of such a little celebration. A little Christmas play or the performance of a song or even just dressing the children up as Mary, an angel, or a shepherd, belong to the Christmas happiness of children.

The tradition of the Advent calendar can be transformed also into the tradition of a Christmas calendar for the twelve or thirteen (including January 6) days. Here it would be appropriate to have little bags filled with 'precious stones', crystals and similar beautiful natural objects. For somewhat older children an art-postcard calendar is also to be recommended.

The Christmas presents, the very number of which is sometimes overwhelming, can be spread out over the twelve days to the benefit of the celebration of the Christmas days. Then, in the morning or at the evening celebration, particularly on Sundays, and holidays like New Year's Day and New Year's Eve another little package is suddenly discovered under the tree. But not every day, so that greed or the feeling that one is entitled to such presents does not arise.

A postcard calendar

The postcard calendar is a very beautiful and stimulating idea for older children. On a large piece of golden cardboard twelve postcards with Christmas motifs are attached. They could be placed in a sequence revealing a common theme from the annunciation to the three kings. The individual cards are covered by a double door made from lightweight gold paper. The wings of the door are cut a little bit higher and wider than the cards and are glued to the cardboard on the right and on the left next to the card. The doors are then closed with a little gold star. Every day beginning on December 25 one door can be opened and the wings rolled back to the sides. To illustrate the connection between the twelve days of Christmas and the twelve months of the year, we could choose instead cards which picture the cycle of the festivals of the year. For example:

January	Worship of the kings
February	From Jesus Christ's life on earth, for instance the Temptation or the Transfiguration
March	A cross
April	Resurrection
May	Ascension
June	Pentecost (also known as Whitsun)
July	John the Baptist or the Baptism the Jordan
August	Christ and his disciples
September	A healing
October	A picture of St Michael
November	A motif from the Apocalypse, or ten maidens with the Lamps
December	Annunciation

Another meaningful variation is possible if the course of the year of nature is the central theme and the twelve cards are assembled to convey something of the mood of each month. Pictures by Caspar David Friedrich, Van Gogh, the Impressionists and other modern painters are good examples which capture the moods of nature. The twelve days of Christmas were experienced in earlier times as a 'year within the year'. Some considered even the weather on these days as prophetic of the coming twelve months.

Looking at the cards together can give us an opportunity for discussions with the children. Because the doors can be flattened and closed again the calendar can be decorated with new cards and used again and again over the years.

Transparencies

Colored tissue transparencies are some of the most meaningful decorations of Advent and Christmas time. The joy of handcrafting transparencies is one of the many games and activities which seem to appear by themselves at certain times of the year and then again disappear. Transparencies can be made by children of various ages and abilities. (Many suggestions for such work are found in the book, *Advent for Children*, by Freya Jaffke.) When placed in a window or in front of another source of light, a transparency appears illuminated from within, so to speak. The most wonderful experiences of this kind are offered to us by Gothic cathedrals with their beautiful stained glass windows. The external light, which otherwise floods through these windows, illuminates in these images of spiritual truths. The light carries these truths to us. As

Goethe said, colors are 'deeds and suffering of light'. When illuminated 'from behind' we experience other qualities of color. More is revealed to us than when the light merely shines upon them. In the northern hemisphere this experience is particularly appreciated in the darkest times of the year; from Advent to Christmas.

4 Epiphany

Epiphany, also called Three Kings time begins on January 6. Four Sundays with their weeks belong to it. January 6 once possessed a significance reaching far beyond our present Christmas festival.

Two significant events are united on this day. The first, the three priest-kings, Melchior, Balthazar and Caspar, brought their offerings in worship to the Jesus child (Matt.2:12–12). The kings had seen a star rise and led by it had found the place where the child was. The second, thirty years later, John the Baptist performed the Baptism of Jesus of Nazareth in the Jordan River. John the Baptist became the witness of the actual birth of Christ at this Baptism for he saw 'how the spheres of heaven opened and the spirit of God in the form of a dove descended and entered him' (Matt.3:16 author's translation). And the voice from heaven which John heard in this special moment said, 'You are my son, the beloved, in whom I reveal myself'. In Luke's Gospel this moment is recorded and an important addition is heard in the words, 'Today I have begotten thee'. The three years on earth of the Son of

God began with the Baptism in the Jordan, with the birth of Christ in Jesus of Nazareth.

'Epiphany', 'appearance', is what this time is called. The word comes from the Greek *epiphaneia* which means to shine above or shine over. The star which the three kings saw was not to be found in the visible sky. The important constellations of that time were like a prophetic indication of this important spiritual event awaited by the wise of all the great pre-Christian cultures. The 'star' which they experienced was the spiritual being of the divine son shining over the child on the earth. This 'star' united with Jesus of Nazareth at the Baptism in the River Jordan. The poet Novalis speaks about this star in one of the verses of his 'Spiritual Songs', 'He is the star, He is the sun, He is eternal life begun . . .' January 6, Epiphany Day combines both of these events.

The manger

The manger, so often loved by the little children should remain during the Epiphany time for awhile, but should undergo a few changes. The manger scene could be changed significantly with the following alterations. Mary, Joseph and child remain. If possible, Mary receives a delicate golden crown or circlet around her head and holds the child in her arms. The three kings (Melchior with a red cloak offering gold; Balthazar in blue, with incense, and Caspar, the dark king, in green, offering myrrh) are grouped around the mother and child. The innumerable portrayals of this scene often display Mary like a queen on a throne with a golden crown on her head. Mary is not only humble and devoted, but she also displays an inner regality of the soul. The twelve days of Christmas can be integrated symbolically in the Epiphany manger. The Christmas tree, the stall or the house in which the manger is located disappear secretly overnight. In their place on the morning of Three Kings' Day twelve burning candles, one for each day of Christmas, stand in a half circle on the festival table, like a cloak of light around the manger scene. The fact that the Christmas tree is now missing will not be experienced so much by the children as a loss or emptiness, but rather a new festival experience is awakened. In order to take up the theme of the star which is so important at this time, a beautiful large star on a cloth (perhaps in a regal reddish-purple) can be placed behind the manger shining over it. One could also partake of a star oneself! In the morning a star cookie, baked with the children's help, can be placed on every breakfast plate.

We can then tell the small children the Gospel story in our own words; the Gospel itself can be read to school-age children, though without the slaying of the innocents.

Perhaps the kings have even brought a present for the children which has been saved for this moment, for example, from the godparents. Children like to become kings themselves wearing a gold crown and colored cloth as a cloak. Then it is easy to improvise a short Three Kings' play.

If the construction of the manger figures permits it (with figures permanently kneeling it will not be possible), one can consider changing the manger scene during the Holy Nights, making use of the entire room. Gradually, the shepherds return to their flocks after Christmas and perhaps by New Year's Day they have disappeared entirely. However, the three kings now appear in the Christmas room, indeed in three different places! Every morning they move a little closer to the manger and eventually they meet and travel the last distance together. On the morning of January 6 they arrive at the manger. If they can carry a gift, then the red king, Melchior, can offer his gold. The next day the blue king, Balthazar, takes his turn with the incense, and on the third day Caspar, the dark king, will offer the child his myrrh. The angel tells them in a dream to return to their land by another way. Mary and Joseph then set out with the child on their way toward Egypt. If we decide to shape the festival in this way it is very important that the paths the kings take through the room are worthily

44

prepared and that the children do not play with the manger figures. The movement forward occurs, of course, secretly. Also older children who are already 'in the know', like to immerse themselves in the process, especially when younger siblings are involved.

Saint Christopher

Since the Epiphany season lasts for four weeks it is best to remove the manger scene after a while so that it doesn't gradually become a mere decoration. A good length of time would be from January 6 through the following Sunday until the Saturday after that. To replace this scene we can use a figure much loved by children, St Christopher. This is the giant man who searched for the greatest lord in the world, finding him in the form of a small child whom he carried through the raging torrent of a river. The complete legend is suitable for telling in the second grade (age 8). But it is quite appropriate for a picture of the Christ-bearer to hang above the festival table. Like the kings, Offerus, or Reprobus as he is sometimes named, also seeks a path to the lord of the entire world. His following of the star is, to be sure, not yet illuminated by the bright light of knowledge; nevertheless, he is led so assuredly in the depths of his soul that he seeks and serves for a long time (also encountering evil on his path just as the kings did), until he finally reaches the right lord. So St Christopher has a certain entitlement to replace the king's manger scene. For ultimately all of mankind should, as Goethe said, become 'like a king on a pilgrimage towards this goal'. The purple color cloth and the star should remain for the whole four weeks on the festival table.

There is a wonderful Christopher play from the great pedagogue, Caroline von Heydebrand. There are two verses from this play which are quite appropriate for reciting with the children. Upon awakening in the morning Offerus meets an angel who speaks to him:

> Offerus, seek the strongest Lord
> Offerus, follow the brightest star
> Offerus, seek the highest good
> In reverence and in will to serve.

And Offerus answers him:

> I will seek the strongest Lord
> I will follow the brightest star
> I will work for the highest good
> As my angel will guide me

One can speak these verses with the child as in a dialogue. It is also possible, and an impressive experience for the child, if in place of the name Offerus, the child's own first name is spoken.

5 Passiontide and Holy Week

Great restraint is required when introducing children to Passiontide and Holy Week. Younger children under nine should not yet take any conscious part in them. They have not matured enough in their development that they could experience the great sacrificial death of the Son of God become man, the death which affects and transforms mankind and the earth. Children have an absolute and direct relationship to the resurrected Christ, who is always present, and to his words 'I am with you always to the close of the age' (Matt. 28:20). The self-knowledge which belongs to Passiontide and which adults go through at this time of year as an inner experience of suffering is simply not appropriate for children. Conscious immersion into the depths of Christ's suffering unto death should not be initiated before the time of preparation for Confirmation (age 14).

Just as Advent prepares Christmastide through four Sundays and weeks, so the four weeks of Passiontide, the last week of which is Holy Week, prepare for Easter. The festival table, though remaining in the 'quiet background', should be decorated suitably. For the reasons mentioned above it is not appropriate to include a representation of Christ on the cross. Anyone who feels it necessary to have some sign of the cross will find outstanding examples among the Celtic or Langobardian stone crosses which are even appropriate for children; one could design a batik following some of these cross forms. A green cloth background is particularly appropriate for such representations. Under the cross stands a vase, perhaps with branches whose buds gradually open and develop into leaves — an experience for the children to follow. In this way the realm of nature is again added to the festival. And if then an empty bowl stands on the table which remains empty during the entire time, then one has the appropriate symbol for Passiontide.

Appropriate fairy tales

There are many fairy tales involving motifs which can be appropriately told during Passiontide appears. Most especially these include stories in which people must go through suffering, enchantment or death.* 'The Wolf and the Seven Little Kids', in which disobedience leads to disaster; 'Little Red Riding Hood', in

* Something of the background to fairy tales can be found in Rudolf Meyer's *Wisdom of Fairy Tales*.

which demonic forces want to swallow the child in man; 'Snow White', where evil calls forth the weaknesses in the human soul and leads it astray. 'The Donkey' (St Francis for example named the body 'brother donkey'). We all must suffer under the limitations which it places upon our true self. Another Passiontide story is 'King Thrushbeard' which shows how the human soul must find the path from proud arrogance to genuine humility through the experience of suffering.

The movable date of Easter

Easter day, the beginning of the Easter season, is determined by celestial events. It is actually read from the heavens. For Easter to be celebrated the spring equinox, the day when the length of the day and night are equal, must have passed. Thereafter, we must wait for the full moon. The first Sunday after this first full moon of spring is Easter Sunday. Passiontide therefore presents a good opportunity to direct the attention of older children to the heavens. They can thus begin to realize how great cosmic laws affect our earthly lives.

Holy Week

Since the fourth century, Holy Week has also been called the 'Great Week' or the 'Quiet

Week'. The events of each day of Holy Week lend a special quality to the corresponding days of the week throughout the year. It would be premature to bring the events of Holy Week to the attention of younger children. However, what parents are able to observe and understand with a reverent mood of gratitude will be sensed and absorbed by the children. The quiet seriousness which is cultivated during these days will be perceived with their clear feeling.

There are some preparations for the Easter festival in which children can take part without being prematurely brought into the Easter experience. For example, the Easter nest can be prepared on the festival table to await its Easter fulfillment. One commendable custom is to sow seeds of grass or summer wheat on Palm Sunday in a small flowerpot. The seeds are covered with a thin layer of soil, 'buried', so to speak. For a few days nothing can be seen; then, however, out of the dark earth delicate points of green break forth. In John's Gospel (12:26–26) Christ compares the seed dying in the earth from which a new plant comes forth to himself, as a parable for his own sacrificial death and resurrection.

Another old custom worthy of being revived is the tradition of baking shaped Easter bread. We can twist and form shapes with special meaning out of yeast dough. Here the children really like to help. On Easter morning carefully shaped baked bread appears on each breakfast plate and on the festival table stands a little basket of the same for guests.

There is something which we should avoid doing with the children until their ninth year, as tempting as it may be. The children should not be the ones who color the eggs which will be found on Easter morning. In our lean, 'street-wise' times it is all too tempting to reveal all secrets to children. The origin of those wonderfully colored eggs should remain one of childhood's mysteries.

When the children become older, (beginning around the twelfth year) we can begin to introduce them to a few events of Holy Week. *The Three Years*, by Emil Bock, helps parents experience the days of Holy Week. Much thereof can be told to the children. The questions which may then arise can be answered out of the background provided by this book.

Art postcards which portray the various motifs of Holy Week also have a place on the festival table. One can add one each day until a complete picture of Holy Week stands on the table. The events of the individual days of Holy Week are as follows:

Palm Sunday: The entry into Jerusalem

Monday: The cursing of the fig tree; the cleansing of the Temple

Tuesday:	The debates in the Temple; (the 'little Apocalypse', Luke 21)
Wednesday:	The anointing of Jesus by Mary Magdalene; the betrayal by Judas
Maundy Thursday:	The washing of the feet; the Last Supper, the discourse
Good Friday:	The Passion in Gethsemane; the capture; the trial and condemnation; the bearing of the cross and the crucifixion; laying in the grave
Holy Saturday:	Christ in the realm of the dead

6 Easter

In the early days of Christianity Easter was the most important festival. Today it still is in the Eastern Church. It is because of Easter Sunday that Sunday is so important in our time. There is a certain glow of the first resurrection day shining above every Sunday. We can choose from a wealth of traditions and symbols for celebrating Easter which have been handed down over the centuries. Many are so meaningful that it is worthwhile to readopt them or to re-enliven them for modern use.

The word Easter probably comes from the Anglo-Saxon name *Eostrae*, Old High German *Ostara*. According to the Venerable Bede (around AD 700) a German spring and light goddess was so named. Also the word 'aurora', the morning dawn, is a cognate word. The resurrection of Christ in the morning, 'as the sun rose,' is the beginning of a new creation, of new life, of new working of light within the old creation.

The Easter egg

Children live for days in joyful anticipation of the search for eggs on Easter morning. Nevertheless, we should perhaps first gather the children together at the Easter festival table when they enter the room. With an Easter candle already burning on the table we can then sing an Easter song, perform music, recite a verse for Easter, and so on. Then, after this contemplation one can allow them the joy of egg searching.

The egg has a significant task at Easter. The content which it symbolizes is not new. It is of central significance in the creation myths of various peoples. For example, in Ancient India, it was told that the earth and heavens came into being out of a golden egg which shone like the sun and split into two halves. The Persians imagined the original world, untouched by evil, as a gigantic egg of light. According to an old nature myth of the Egyptians, the first god evolved out of an egg. Similarly, the belief was customary that the sun god arose from an egg 'as the infant of eightfoldness'. Also the inner sarcophagus in which a mummy rested was designated an egg. In the Greek concept of the world's creation, the great goddess and primal mother Nyx laid a silver egg. From that emerged a god with golden wings: Eros, the god of love, the firstborn. He brought

everything hidden in the silver egg into the light. Also the Finnish creation myths know of a golden egg which finally breaks into two halves. Heaven and earth arise from the two shells, and the golden yolk begins to shine as the sun.

Eggs have also been found in graves from pre-Christian times. In the Pergamon Museum in Berlin there is an ostrich egg on display which was laid in a grave in Babylon around the eighth century BC. Many peoples of ancient times practiced this custom. Even today, in many places in Greece the custom of placing a red egg on graves at Easter is still alive. An egg laid on a grave was meant to be a seed of hope for new life.

The egg has become the symbol of resurrection for Christians. New life breaks through the hard shell; this is possible because in every egg a golden sun, the egg yolk, is hidden. The egg is therefore not only a symbol for the beginning of the world, but also for a new beginning of creation which can be brought to life in every human being through the resurrection of Christ. The apostle Paul said in his Letter to the Galatians (2:20) concerning his deepest experience of Christ, 'it is no longer I who live, but Christ who lives in me.' When we have children hunt Easter eggs, we associate with this act our wish that they may likewise seek access to the inner power of resurrection in their lives

and that they may find it. An Armenian illuminated manuscript (from AD 1038) shows
clearly the symbolic connection between the
egg and the resurrection. The women have
come to the grave. The grave is empty and the
angel sitting upon it appears to speak the words
of the Gospel, 'He is not here, he is resurrected.' These words are not actually written in
the usual way as a band of words across the
page, but are implied by the finger of the angel
pointing to a large white egg.

Decorating eggs

There are plenty of ideas in many crafts books
concerning the decoration of eggs. But, here it
is good to ask oneself again the question, Why?
Why do we decorate and color Easter eggs? At
one time they were given white. Again the
Greek language helps us further. The Greek
word for decoration is cosmos. Cosmos
signified at the same time 'order', the 'world',
and the 'order of the world'. The opposite of
cosmos is chaos. The small world of the Easter
egg is, through its decoration, given its place in
the larger order of world harmony. The forms
of circles, spirals, triangles, squares, wavy
lines, meanders, blossoms and stars, lines from
pole to pole, and twisted bands all indicate such
a connection.

Even coloring an egg with only one color

clothes it in a decorative covering. The radiant colors have a direct effect on the soul and are at the same time an expression of it. In the color and the style of our clothing we reveal outwardly something which lives inwardly in us.

The most outstanding color of Easter is red, and therefore the Easter hare should place a red Easter egg on the bowl of green grass or grain planted on Palm Sunday. On Grunewald's resurrection painting of the Isenheim Altar, the Resurrected One brings forth from the grave a winding cloth with a rich spectrum of colors, which seem to shine from within. The re-enlivening of the human soul can emanate from the Easter event. We reveal something of this fact to the child through the joyfully radiant colors of the Easter egg.

The Easter hare

The Easter hare brings or hides the Easter eggs. One should not confuse him with the rabbit or bunny (with the Jack Rabbit or Bunny Rabbit). They are his good friends; but he himself is invisible and has, of course, a golden pelt. So that the Easter hare can really come, the grown-ups must know him a little and be convinced of his mythical value.

The hare is a herbivore which does not harm other animals. On the contrary, there are sufficient credible reports that these animals even intercede for one another and that one hare chased by a dog can be given a break while another hare jumps in for it. This fact in itself would suffice to attribute to the animal its great symbolic value. Yet, there are still other motifs. The hare has, as opposed to a little rabbit, no burrows in which to hide. It lives with a certain homelessness. Or, seen from another point of view, its home is everywhere. The hare in some areas is called 'Master Lamp'. He was experienced as a light bringer who lit the lamps. This name indicates his association with the Germanic spring and light (moon!) goddess, whose messenger and companion was supposed to have been the hare.

The long and beautiful ears with which the hare can hear so well are very delicate and sensitive. In German, hunters call these ears 'spoons'. With a spoon we can take up something of delicate consistency. The resurrection of the Logos, the Word of God, as Christ is also named, is, despite its greatness, not a fact that must overwhelm human consciousness. Only if we approach this fact with reverence will we be able to understand it and to experience the new creative word in ourselves. At the same time ears are organs of wakefulness, organs for perceiving the many enemies of the hare.

What child — and what adult — is not delighted to see hares on the edge of the woods, and to observe their upright stance, a playful reaching for the human power of uprightness. The hare also plays an important role in pre-Christian and Christian cultures, in their philosophy, literature, and art.

All of these individual motifs together cause the hare to become the Easter hare, to become the archetypal mythical picture, a symbol of the self which has overcome personal egotism and is capable of devotion and sacrifice. The Easter hare does not lay the egg, the seed for a new creation through the resurrection of Christ, but he is permitted to bring it.

That the celebration of the Easter festival has gradually become encumbered through the ever-increasing world of commerce is apparent. Strictly considered, the Easter hare should not bring anything besides eggs; actually, not even anything sweet.

Seeking and finding eggs is for all of the children a fun and important Easter experience. As human beings we can actually only seek something if we are aware of or at least suspect its existence. The Easter report of Luke's Gospel (24:5–5) treats the motif of seeking in a special way. The women are seeking the body which was laid in the grave but they do not find it. The angel's answer to this seeking is, 'Why do you seek the living among the dead?' The effort was correct but its direction was wrong. There is much more that could be said concerning seeking which is found in the Gospel. Perhaps it suffices here to quote the central sentence, 'Seek and you will find', (Matt. 7:7). A conscious act of seeking which occurs out of inner freedom is the foundation for all spiritual striving. 'Anyone who cannot seek like a determined suitor, remains bound by deception of sevenfold veils' (Christian Morgenstern). Through seeking Easter eggs we can convey to the children the Easter impulse: seek him, you will find him.

The festival table

As a background for the resurrection picture a piece of red cloth, cardboard, or construction paper can be placed behind the table. On the table covered with a green cloth, stands the bowl or, if there are many children, the bowls, with the sprouting seeds, and red egg, and the bowl with the breads of various shapes. The empty bowl of Passiontide awaits its fulfillment with the Easter eggs which will soon be found. A large white candle burns which can be lit on each of the forty days of Easter. One can also include a vase with green or blossoming branches. On these or other bouquets of branches the children are permitted to hang their own decorated eggs. The Easter tree can also be located here.

The Easter 'tree'

From the wealth of customs available we can adopt an old one, almost forgotten, and re-enliven it: the Easter tree corresponding to the Christmas tree. Remembering the legend of paradise, we can give new reasons for this old custom.

After the expulsion from paradise, Seth, the third son of Adam and Eve, was allowed once again to enter. Adam, upon his death, had asked him to go. With the help of the archangel Michael, Seth gained entrance into paradise and saw how the two trees, the Tree of Knowledge and the Tree of Life had grown together in their crowns. After they had eaten from the Tree of Knowledge Adam and Eve had been forced to leave paradise so that they could no longer eat from the Tree of Life. Seth obtained the seeds from these trees which had grown together, and placed them in the coffin with Adam's body. According to the legend, the cross on Golgotha was made from the wood of the tree that grew out of these seeds in Adam's grave. From this cross of death comes new life for the world. For the cross is for Christians not only the sign of sacrificial death but also the sign of Christ resurrected.

The stark, clear form of the Easter tree reminds one clearly of the cross. The four cross-beam branches decorated with green as well as the eggs hanging upon them remind one of the new life. The eggs can also express in their color that Easter is a festival of world renewal, as the poet Novalis called it, a festival in which the entire first creation takes part. The eggs can be decorated with the colors of the four elements.

earth	purple
water	blue
air	yellow
fire	red

Other symbols can also decorate the Easter tree. Figures baked from dough: one or two human beings (man and woman, Adam and Eve) standing at foot of the tree; on the middle axis above them, a cock, and all the way at the top the sun.

The cock, through its particular sensitivity to light, is the awakener for the coming day. In Christian symbolism he is a picture for the human 'I' or ego. Peter, who denied the Lord, was awakened again to himself by the third crow of the cock (Luke 22:62–62). The church father Ambrosius (fourth century) says concerning the cock, 'The cock calls those who are lying to rise, and scolds the sleepyheads.' 'Hope returns at the crow of the cock.'

In the fairy tale 'The Bremen Town Musicians' the cock stands at the top above the donkey, dog and cat. We can see the cock as a symbol for the wakeful self above all the rest; the 'I' of the wakeful human is capable of perceiving the rising sun of Christ.

Easter time lasts for forty days until the festival called Christ's Ascension. It is not at first easy to carry and cultivate the Easter atmosphere through forty days. With time however, we can gradually come to experience Easter more and more. Practice helps, and from year to year we can perceive a growing ability in this regard. An Easter festival table can help us in this task with a visible reminder.

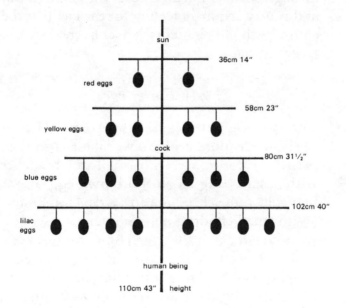

Easter water

The Easter water custom is good for children from around six years. Early on Easter morning, perhaps even at sunrise, they arise in silence and go silently to a well or spring, and fill a vessel with 'Easter water', and say a verse, or sing a song.

We are dealing here not with magical actions (one can simply use the water for the house plants afterwards) but rather with an experience of the holiness of the word awakened through silence. Furthermore, the children can in this way acquire a feeling for the fact that the entire earth, all elements, are enlivened by the Easter event.

Forty Easter eggs

The growing power of the forty days of Easter can be made more visible if we take a large vase, perhaps a floor vase with small tree branches within, and hang a colorful blown egg on the branches on each of the forty days of Easter. (With small children not yet attending school, we need not count the eggs.) Since the resurrection is an event of the early morning, the eggs should also be hung early in the morning. Decorating eggs for the tree is a wonderful task which the children can do throughout Easter time. The most beautiful eggs can be saved for use again next year. In this way parents can collect a small treasure in the course of the years. Later when the children are grown and gone from the home these Easter eggs may be more precious than ever

Suggestions for the forty days

Among the fairy tales, particularly those of the Brothers Grimm and the Russian stories, are several with an Easter-like character. Actually, all fairy tales and legends with motifs of transformation, overcoming death and redemption are Easter stories. For example, 'The Frog King', 'Rapunzel', 'The Two Brothers', 'The Crystal Ball' (here the egg appears too). Beginning with age nine the following are appropriate: the story of Tobias (in the Apocrypha to the Old Testament), Flor and Blanchiflor. Beginning with twelve years: Parsival. These stories can be divided up over several days, Parsival over several weeks. If the stories are told with the Easter candle burning the connection with Easter is obvious for the child.

In addition to painting blown eggs, one can braid, weave, fold paper or work with clay on rainy afternoons. Here, too, there are innumerable possibilities. Braiding or weaving has a kind of cosmic ordering as its basic principle. Folding has a transformative principle and working with clay uses the principle of forming and shaping. This is Easter activity all the way down into the hands! However, children should only be introduced to these activities when they have reached the appropriate age. These should all be activities of creative joy and not great effort for them.

Outdoors one can play ball (throwing the curve of the sun) and swing (to experience the air). It is good if the child can be given a small plot of earth for sowing and planting in his own garden. Easter time is a very good time for taking walks with our children. All these Easter activities acquire a special significance when accompanied by adults having an inner understanding of the spiritual background. It is good if during these days the child can experience the essence of all four elements: earth, air, fire and water; of the earth through clay modeling and gardening, of water through collecting Easter water, of the air through playing ball and swinging, through making little windmills and with fire through the Easter candle. If we can celebrate the Easter season anew it will become for us a source of joy and confidence in life.

7 Ascension

The forty days of Easter lead to the festival
called Ascension (Acts 1:12–12). With this
experience, the resurrected Christ grows
beyond his disciples ' ability to perceive him.
Unable to follow him with their human
consciousness they are only aware of a great
loss. But, he does not really depart from the
earth but rather becomes Lord of all the heavenly forces working upon earth. In this way he
brings the forces achieved through his
resurrection into the body of the earth and
humanity. This is described in Luke's Gospel
with a picture of Christ being raised up to
heaven while blessing those around him
(24:53–53). Blessing the world, radiating his
substance, the Resurrected One unites his
being with heaven, with the earth, and with
man.

The festival table

In the art of the Middle Ages, particularly in
manuscript illustration, there are many
impressive representations of Ascension. From
their meditations, the illustrators (who were

often monks) managed to achieve paintings of great expression. A small print of one of these paintings could be hung on gold cardboard above the table. The table can be covered with a green cloth. A white candle is also present, perhaps the Easter candle still. A bouquet of colorful meadow flowers stands next to the candles. The blossom's opening itself to heaven as a gesture of nature is very appropriate at this festival. To create for the child a picture of the stream of blessings which come to the earth because of Ascension we can place on the green cloth below the bouquet many small golden stars. Heavenly forces have now come to the earth.

The clouds

Ascension is bound up with the image of clouds: 'a cloud took him out of their sight' (Acts 1:9). The clouds visible in the sky are a parable for the process which occurred there.* Often during the ten days of Ascension the sky even shows us many impressive cloud formations. During walks with the children on these days, we can take the time to consciously observe the clouds, and to ponder their nature, their ability to range over and exceed all

* See also *Ascension*, by Friedrich Benesch for a full description of the intimate connection between the clouds the festival.

boundaries. The changing forms of the cloud structures can stimulate our imaginative faculties in a powerful and wonderful way.

Dandelion puffs

What child does not love the dandelion with its many golden, sunlike blossoms! On an Ascension walk with the children, we can let the children pick dandelion puffs and blow the seeds with their little stars into the wide world. This works best when done from a small hilltop with a slight wind blowing. The festival of Ascension is threatened with extinction through neglect. Yet, all those who have experienced, even a little bit, the greatness of this ten-day festival will want to do all they can to plant in the hearts of the children a seed of understanding for the tremendous meaning of this festival.

8 Whitsun

The word Whitsun, meaning 'white Sunday', comes from the tradition of wearing white baptismal dresses at the festival of Whitsun, or Pentecost. The word 'Pentecost' comes from the Greek and means the fiftieth (day after Easter). As described in the Acts of the Apostles (2:1), the disciples were together on this day and united in heart and mind. Into the harmony of their thoughts, feelings and common religious practice, came the gift of inspiration from the Holy Spirit. In the great rushing flow of joy in their souls they were enlightened with the knowledge: Christ is united with each and every one of us in the deepest way possible; he has not disappeared – he is here. Being thus inspired, that is, 'in-spirited' the disciples were able to go out and proclaim to the people gathered what had occurred and bring about a similar experience in them. Whitsun is a festival of Christian community. A human being who has been touched in his heart by the being of Christ will always seek out his fellow brothers and sisters to share with them the presence of Christ.

The festival table

Wherever Christ's Ascension is portrayed in art, usually Whitsun is also pictured. Above the heads of the disciples we see the tongues of fire. Sometimes Mary is portrayed as a representative of the human soul in the middle. Such a Whitsun picture deserves a place above the festival table. Again there is a white candle on the table. At Whitsun there should be a further circle of twelve candles around the one in the middle, which should be a little longer and larger than the others. The twelve candle holders could be made by the children out of clay at Easter time and painted perhaps in twelve different colors. Flowers are particularly well suited as nature's contribution. Daisies or other flowers belonging to the composite family, that is plants whose blossoms are composed of many flowerlets growing together on a central disk, are best. These are flowers actually consisting of many individual blossoms which spring from a common base.

The lighting of candles

On Whitsun morning when the children come into the room, the middle candle should already be burning. After a song and a verse each child is permitted, also each grown-up, to light a candle from the middle one. The children can then light the extra candles for others who are connected with them, perhaps for grand-parents, or godparents, friends and relatives, or those who might be ill or have passed away. The child thus experiences a community of people surrounding him for whom it is also permitted to do things. The little word 'for' is one of the most precious words we possess as human beings striving to be Christians.

The lighting of the candles should occur on at least three days, the first time on the morning of Whitsunday, perhaps on Whitmonday, if it is a holiday, and on the following Sunday. Again and again, new people can be taken into the circle of those for whom the candles are lit. This deed of lighting candles for others can later grow into prayer for other people.

Stories

Fairy tales suitable for Whitsun include 'Cinderella': the doves (a symbolic picture for the Holy Spirit) help the prince to distinguish between good and evil, and to know who the true bride is.

'The Three Languages': from the wisdom of doves the Holy Mass can be read.

Beginning around age ten the Grail story of Lohengrin is also very appropriate for children. (The knight on the swan who was sent from the Grail brings peace and freedom to the threatened human soul and the people.) The story is easily divided into several sections for reading.

9 Saint John's Tide

After the summer solstice, on June 24, we celebrate St John's Day, the birthday of John the Baptist. This day begins St John's Tide, which in The Christian Community is celebrated for the four following Sundays.

John the Baptist was the one who prepared the way for Christ. He serves this function still today. His powerful flaming sermons have lost nothing of their immediacy. The essential and constantly repeated motif in his sermons is contained in the words 'Change your thinking!' and 'Prepare the way of the Lord!' The way in which the inner soul of man is to be prepared is indicated in a quote from the prophet Isaiah: 'As it is written in the book of the words of Isaiah the prophet, "the voice of one crying in the wilderness: Prepare the way of the Lord, make his paths straight. Every valley shall be filled, and every mountain and hill shall be brought low, and the crooked shall be made straight, and the rough ways shall be made smooth"' (Luke 3:4f). Mountains and valleys are not only external objects of nature, they also picture conditions within the soul. We experience them in the life of feelings, as we swing between the heights of jubilant ecstasy to the depths of depression and despair. The task of John is to hold the balance between these two extremes. Furthermore, the 'crooked' ways of thinking are to be led into clarity and the hindrances which again and again paralyze the will are to be gradually eliminated through disciplined spiritual work. Of course, we cannot bring the flaming words of John to the children, at least not their content. However, there is a picture which speaks to us of the path of inner development. This path can be characterized by the lily and the rose.

The lily and the rose

The lily and the rose are visible representatives of opposites. If we look at the lily we see a bulb plant whose design clearly follows the principle of three. Barely rooted in the kingdom of the earth, it shows no noticeable transformation of shape in the leaves. Two triangles form the six-pointed star of its blossom. The six-pointed star is the star of annunciation. The principle of the lily reveals itself directly. This fact, combined with the pure white of the blossom, caused the flower to be seen as a symbol of the heavenly paradisal innocence of man. The pure white lily is, so to speak, the flower of the beginning. We are reminded here of pictures of the annunciation of the archangel Gabriel to Mary, in which the lily is often included for this symbolic message.

The rose is very different as we can readily see. It is powerfully rooted in the earth. Its form underlies a clearly recognizable principle of five, the five-pointed star, the pentagram. The five-pointed star is the star of fulfillment. In the transformations which the plant undergoes, this principle is clearly revealed: in the leaves, in the position of the leaves on the stem, and in its blossom, whether in the pure simple blossom of the wild rose or in the manifold beauty of the cultivated rose. The words of Schiller are particularly well-suited to this wonderful plant once ennobled by the knowledge of man,

'Do you seek the highest, the greatest? The plant can teach it to you.

This is it: What the plant is without trying, you be through effort.' If we desire inner transformation, then we have achieved consciously the level which the plant lives without consciousness. Then we are living according to the intentions of John. The goal of mankind cannot be reached through the simplicity of a 'back to the lily!' attitude but rather through developing into the future. The rose is the picture for this development.

For people who meditate, the rose has been a particularly important symbol ever since the

Middle Ages. Goethe even goes beyond this 'personal' significance of the rose. In the second part of his great drama, Faust, (Act 5) there is a struggle for the soul of Faust who has just died. The decisive turning point occurs when a blossoming rose branches drive away the demonic spirits.

> THE YOUNGER ANGEL: From fair
>   sinners' hands these flowers,
> Roses have we scattered wide:
> Thus they made the victory ours,
> Penitent and purified;
> Flowers this soul, this prize have won us.

The power to overcome here represented by the rose helped to drive away the forces of evil. These roses came out of the hands of loving, holy penitents. Later in the drama these penitents appear again as three women: Mary Magdalene (Magna Peccatrix), the Samaritan woman at the well (Mulier Samaritana), and Maria Aegyptica. Each one of these women experienced a decisive turning point, a change of thinking in their destinies. They went through guilt and found the way to their true self. They were even able to develop overflowing, 'super-fluous' moral forces which were then available to help others. From their hands came the helpful roses.

Much more could be said here to characterize the archetypal polarity of the lily and the rose.

Perhaps this is enough, however, to stimulate further thought by the reader.

The festival table

The festival table on the morning of St John's Day: On the wall hangs a picture of the Baptist, for example, John the Baptist in the portal of the cathedral at Chartres, or John the Baptist by Leonardo da Vinci; the wise powerful figure of the Baptist of the Isenheim Altar, or others. On the left, next to the picture there stands a white lily, on the right a bouquet of roses, or a single red rose. Between the lily and the rose 'lies' the path which John the Baptist would point out to mankind.

John the Baptist's food

It is reported that John lived from fruits and wild honey while living in the wilderness. We could prepare with the children a similar St John's meal. Many wonderful berries ripen around this time; the many varieties can be served sweetened with a little honey.

Stories for this festival

Of course, the fairy-tale, 'Faithful John', by the Brothers Grimm is a natural for this festival time: the faithful protector who sacrifices himself and prepares the way for the young prince and his bride to true fulfillment.

St John's Tide and Christmas

St John's motif is written above John's hand on the Isenheim Altar: 'He must increase, but I must decrease.' (John 3:30). This motif can also be experienced in the sun's course through the year. At St John's Tide the external sunlight begins to decrease. Exactly a half year later, after the winter solstice, we celebrate Christmas — the birth of the divine sun of the spirit. To create a relationship to Christmas, especially for small children, we can renew the following old custom: we make a bouquet of meadow-herbs and flowers on St John's Day which is then dried (with the blossoms hanging downward) and can appear at Christmas time as hay in the manger. At St John's time so-called strawflowers also bloom. We can pick them in a garden with the children or perhaps buy them in a flower shop. A little bouquet of these flowers should be hung where it can get plenty of air, dry out and wait with the children for Advent and Christmas. Toward the end of St John's time the farmers already begin to harvest. The ears of wheat and other grains lying around on the edges of the field after the harvest can be gathered by the children and also saved for Advent and Christmas. (For example, the Advent garden or for the 'steps'.)

A St John's walk

For adults, St John's Tide is a time of inner struggle, of striving for virtue. In raising children we are also concerned with developing certain virtues. Among these belong: wonder, reverence and gratitude.

A Sunday walk along the ripe fields of grain, while larks jubilate in the air above, can help us lead the child into a healthy devotional mood, into a quiet atmosphere of warm, deep thankfulness for the gifts of nature. It is, of course, absolutely necessary for the parents themselves to develop this mood of soul; only then can it be imitated by the children. A verse by Rudolf Steiner for children expresses the atmosphere of a St John's Tide walk.

> Sunlight is flooding
> The widths of space
> The song of the birds echoes
> Through the realms of the air
> The blessing of plants sprouts
> From the being of earth
> And human souls lift themselves
> In feelings of thankfulness
> To the Spirits of the World.

10 Michaelmas

Since the ninth century, September 29 has been celebrated as St Michael's Day. In The Christian Community it is celebrated along with St John's Tide, not only as a single day, but as a festival period lasting four weeks. The archangel Michael is of particular significance for our time. Hans-Werner Schroeder says: 'Michael works today not at the level of an archangel but rather at the level of an archai, as the inspiring spirit of our present age, as the leading inspiration for our culture. He has risen for a time from the realm of the archangels to a higher perspective, so to speak, and is equipped to place his all encompassing power in the service of mankind, as a whole and not only for a single people.'

One of Michael's special tasks is inspiring humanity with the power to recognize the reality of the spiritual, so that gradually man will come to experience the spirit and allow it to become the working effective force in human deeds.

A worthy form of celebrating Michaelmas remains to be found in the future. Realizing this, we must nevertheless make the modest attempt to create something for the children which can awaken in them a feeling for the being and working of Michael.

The festival table

It should not be hard to find a picture for the festival table, as there is a wealth of portrayals of Michael. Surveying the various portrayals of the archangel we find a wide spectrum of motifs which, when taken together, provide a fairly complete picture of his essence and his influence. For example: Many pictures show Michael as the dragon-fighter, the dragon sometimes being portrayed as the devil. Michael (the name means 'who is like God') is man's helper, who encourages him in his struggle against evil. The best pictures do not portray the dragon under his feet as dead, but with its overpowering force broken. Michael helps man by creating for him a free space within which his own activity can unfold. This is achieved through his impelling the powers of evil into defined limitations.

Another fundamental motif is seen in Michael with the balancing scale. He appears in this fashion in depictions of the Last Judgment or other scenes which characterize the after-death experience of man. The good and the evil which a soul has done in life are weighed against each other. The soul experiences as pain all that within itself which weighs down the balance of evil, and as blessedness the good which can be attributed to it.

Michael is also often pictured with a transparent world globe in his hand. Usually this globe is marked with a symbolic sign for Christ. This particular Michaelic image indicates his involvement in world history and his dedication towards the building of a new world, the new Jerusalem, as described in the Book of Revelation (21).

Less common portrayals include Michael under the cross of Golgotha, Michael accompanying the soul of the dead, and Michael as the guardian over the portals of churches.

A multitude of pictures show scenes from legends which relate how Michael's deeds help in the destinies of individuals. (The word 'legend' is derived from the Latin word *Leggier*, which means to read. Our word 'legible' also comes from this word. A legend, therefore, must be read with a proper understanding.)

In sum, there is a wealth of pictures from which to choose for the festival table. As the children become older we can change the paintings periodically, so that the various aspects of Michael's being come to the foreground.

The experience of nature during autumn, that of a 'passing away' illuminated by brilliant color, belongs to the Michaelmas festival in the northern hemisphere. Life in nature withdraws expiring in beauty. Standing at the threshold

Michael shows man the way to a higher life, a life lived in conscious union with the spirit. A bouquet of colorful leaves and branches of berries on the table will give us something of this mood.

St Michael's rolls

In all his actions, Michael, a servant of Christ, wants to lead man to an understanding and an experience of Christ and all he has done for us. A few ears of grain on the festival table with a bunch of grapes beneath them can serve as a silent expression of gratitude for the harvest. As the child takes in this arrangement on the festival table a relationship to the deeper secrets of Christianity is gradually awakened in a very gentle way.

In certain parts of Europe there is a custom of eating a Michael's roll or cake on September 29. We can adopt this custom and on Michaelmas Day place a small basked of Michael's rolls (lightly sweetened and with raisins) on the festival table next to the grain and grapes. The children may help with the baking.

The balance

We can renew some of the old customs in celebrating Michaelmas. However, it is especially important at this time to stimulate the chil-

dren's will to do good and involve them in
activities encouraging the good. To this end we
can place a balance on the festival table on the
first morning of the festival. (A balance with
two balance pans is not difficult to make with
simple materials.) One of the balance pans is
weighed down with a large black or darkly colored stone. The child has the task each day of
helping the archangel Michael by placing in the
other balance pan a small stone, a stone perhaps
which was found during a walk or in the garden.
It could be a small white silicate stone or crystal,
one with a beautiful pattern or particular form.
Or the child can take a simple stone and trans-
form it with the help of crayons into a 'precious'
stone. The best time for this little weighing
ceremony is the evening when the day's activities are behind us. The child is then able to see
how the 'good' balance pan becomes heavier
day after day until a state of balance is achieved
and finally the weight of the good is victorious.
Perhaps when the occasion presents itself one
can tell the child that nothing, not even the
smallest good deed, is ever lost, whether or not
it is noticed by anyone. All good deeds are
received by the divine world with joy for they
strengthen the power of good in the world.

In the night after the final day of the festival
(on Saturday after the fourth Sunday) the two
balance pans should be emptied and the stones
disappear. They should not be saved but rather

sought for every year anew. Through the use of the balance, the four weeks of the festival are not experienced as gradually losing their power. Instead a sense for the power that grows is engendered by this little exercise.

Flying kites

This custom fits perfectly with Michaelmas. Older children always like to fly homemade kites when weather permits. A parent's help is often necessary here. It is a wonderful childhood experience to hold a kite floating in the air above firmly in one's hand and then to have to pull it down again. This activity is an enacted symbol of man's holding the forces of evil in his hands.

The dragon underfoot

It is usually easy to find a strangely shaped piece of root while on a walk through the woods. With the help of modeling wax or clay, and a little fantasy, we can make a dragon out of such roots, perhaps even one with several heads. Then out of the same material we can make a St Michael's figure to ride on top of them. It is good for the child to experience the whole family working together on this on a Sunday afternoon. The small sculpture resulting will find its place on the festival table.

Little plays

If a small group of children gather during this time, it is easy to perform fairy tales and legends, using simple costumes. When the story has been told the children are costumed, the plot briefly discussed and the play begins. Sometimes it is best to perform only carefully chosen individual scenes and to tell the story for the parts in between. Helpful suggestions for this activity can be found in *Celebrating the Festivals with Children* by Friedel Lenz. Because the children identify easily and quickly with the roles they play, a careful choice of stories will strengthen the impulse to have the courage to do good, to bring redemption into the world. Such motifs are found in fairy tales such as 'Iron Hans', 'The Devil with the Three Golden Hairs', 'The Drummer', 'The Crystal Ball', 'The Two Brothers' and 'Sleeping Beauty' (all by the Brothers Grimm); 'The King's Daughter in the Flaming Fortress' (by Zaunert), also in many Russian fairy tales.

Celebrating Michaelmas consciously gives the child courage for life and action.

11 Martinmas

St Martin of Tours, who was born in 316, died on November 11 in 397. In early Christianity, the day on which an individual died was celebrated as his *dies natalis*, the 'day of birth' in the divine world. St Martin is known in Christendom as the deeply religious man who shared his cloak with a beggar. He was able to experience the reality of the words, 'as you did to one of the least of these my brethren, you did it to me' (Matt.25:40). Martin has become the representative of the Christian attitude of brotherliness.

When the days become short, the sun goes down earlier, and the stars appear early in the skies, the children according to an old custom, would walk with lanterns through the streets in the early evening singing. This custom is worth renewing — especially if the children can make the lanterns themselves. As the world grows darker the inner light of man wants to shine forth. It is not incidental that the lanterns are often decorated with suns and moons and stars, motifs which also appear in the songs. They suggest heavenly forces which want to live in the souls of human beings on earth.

In many places St Martin's Day is a day when the children would beg for gifts from the people living in the areas where they walked with their lanterns. To fully correspond to the character of Martin, it would be better to encourage the children to give something themselves. Instead of expecting to find the St Martin's attitude in others, it would be better to practice it oneself! There are plenty of old, lonely, ill, or sad people, who would experience a bit of light and warmth from a small greeting brought by the St Martin's Day light-bearers. In the fairy tale, 'The Star Money', there also lives something of the attitude which St Martin practiced.

Above the festival table hangs a picture of Martin and the lanterns wait on the table. In a bowl there is a small sweet 'St Martin's Day bread' for each child. After a St Martin's Day song has been sung, each child should share his bread with someone else.

12 St Nicholas Day

December 6, St Nicholas Day, is awaited by the children with excitement and joy. Many legends have focused on the figure of Nicholas, the bishop of Myra who died in 343. Many varied customs have developed over the years for celebrating this day. Our intention here is not to introduce new customs, but to explain a little those already in practice.

The Golden Legend tells us that Nicholas was born in the city of Patera. His parents were pious and rich people. The father's name was Epiphanius, the mother, Johanna. Already in his childhood Nicholas displayed a deep religious nature which set him apart from others. This led to his being named Bishop of Myra. His actions were characterized by their goodness: he always did what was right, and stood up for the good wherever he found it. In this way he helped people to hold the ship of their lives on the right course. Therefore, Nicholas is also the patron saint of sailors. With his great goodness and determination to support what is right, he has become the one who helps us in our efforts to prepare for Christmas. He praises the children for their good deeds and brings them apples and nuts and lebkuchen (though not yet the Christmas goodies). Sometimes he must also admonish and encourage them to greater efforts. A small switch is a subtle hint in this direction. On the morning of the sixth, each child finds either on a plate or in a cleaned shoe (an indication for the path which should be followed voluntarily), something of this strengthening and admonishment. The parents, as executors of Nicholas ' wishes, can praise the deeds which have made him happy, and, in a loving and kind way, discuss with the child the small weaknesses and misdeeds which were the grounds for the switch, and explain the wishes of St Nicholas in this regard. All this occurs so that the Christ Child can come, that is, so that Christmas can become a real event in the soul. At one time or another the question will arise in every child concerning the 'real' Nicholas. A possible answer satisfying the child and corresponding to the truth would be the following: Nicholas lives in the heavenly world and every year lends to a human being form and voice in order to come to the children. When Nicholas makes a 'personal' appearance, he should not merely be a disguised man. Anyone entrusted with this responsibility must be inwardly genuine and able to identify with his task. The clothing should be worthy and radiate something of the magnitude and greatness of the spiritual world.

Simply experiencing some of the goodness from heaven can be so impressive for a child that it is no longer necessary for St Nicholas to point out any insufficiencies in the child.

13 Halloween and Thanksgiving

by James and Cynthia Hindes

Halloween is one of the most beloved of festivals for children in America and Britain. It has its origin in the Celtic festival of Samhain, which celebrated the first day of winter on November 1. It was believed that the spirits of the dead and other supernatural creatures — fairies, witches, and goblins — spirited about on that night and that the accessibility of the supernatural made it a propitious night for fortune telling. In Ireland a sacred fire for the year was kindled on the altar of their place of worship from which all fires were subsequently lit.

The begging of treats by children probably evolved from the custom of begging peat for the bonfires 'to scare the witches'. Later harvest elements, pumpkins, apples and nuts, were added from the Roman worship of Pomona, the goddess of the harvest, whose festival was around the same time. The Celtic and the Roman elements combined in the jack-o'-lantern, the fire in the pumpkin or turnip.

The name 'Halloween' itself comes from the Christian influence, as the feast is on the eve of All Saints' Day, November 1, making October 31 All Hallow's Eve.

Within the cycle of the Christian year, even though its origins are pagan, Halloween can be experienced as a natural transition from Michaelmas to Martinmas, leading on to Advent. The candle inside the pumpkin or turnip, both fruits of the earth, is like the very last memory and afterglow of the summer sun with its ripening strength. Then for Martinmas a candle is lit within the home-made lantern, this is the first glow of a light with a completely different nature, the first spark of inner light.

In the course of time Halloween has lost much of its depth, yet children experience in a primal way the threatening quality of the growing darkness with a light of its own. We can restore to the festival some of its former harmony and depth by activities which capture the spirit of Halloween. Making costumes, and pumpkin or turnip carving, can themselves be part of the festivities. We can stage a shadow puppet show behind a sheet, enacting a poem, story, or song. We can tell stories, sing songs, bob for apples, but the emphasis of the festival is to find the light in the darkness. It is important that the experience does not become one of gloom or fear.

In England the festival of Guy Fawkes, November 5, with its bonfire and fireworks may well have survived for almost four centuries not so much as an anniversary of a failed plot to blow up Parliament, but because the activity fits with the darkening time of year when we need to find our own light and fire.

Thanksgiving is America's oldest and most universally beloved holiday, celebrated on the fourth Thursday in November. Gratitude, along with reverence and wonder, is one of the three most important attitudes we can help our children to cultivate. The best elements of the Thanksgiving festival with the help of its main motif, the giving of thanks, can elevate it to something which nourishes on many levels.

As a harvest festival we can call to mind all the forces of heaven and earth which have provided us with food, clothing, sustenance. We can remember and thank all who have supported us. Everyone at our Thanksgiving festival could take turns recalling aloud someone or something for which they were thankful.

Bibliography

Benesch, Friedrich, *Ascension*, Floris, Edinburgh 1979.

Frieling, Rudolf, *Das heilige Spiel*, Stuttgart 1925.

Heimeran, Marta, 'Father Christmas', *The Christian Community*, London, December 1934.

Hoerner, Wilhelm, *Zeit und Rhythmus*, Urachhaus, Stuttgart 1978.

Jaffke, Freya, *Advent for Children*, Floris, Edinburgh 1983.

Lenz, Friedel, *Celebrating Festivals with Children*, Anthroposophic, New York 1985.

Meyer, Rudolf, *The Wisdom of Fairy Tales*, Floris, Edinburgh 1988.

Schneider, C. *Der Weihnachtsbaum und seine Heimat, das Elsass*, Philosophisch-Anthroposophisch, Dornach 1977.

Schroeder, Hans-Werner, *Mensch und Engel*, Urachhaus, Stuttgart 1979.

Steiner, Rudolf, *Festivals and Seasons*, (1909), Anthroposophical, London 1928.

——, *Signs and Symbols of the Christmas Festival*, (1906), Anthroposophic, New York 1969.